Hair & Makeup by Sarah Harmer Beauty

Christina is from New Zealand and married with two children. She is founder and fashion designer of her brand Lilika Designs Fashion House.

Featured in world renowned fashion magazines *Cosmopolitan*, *ELLE* and *Harper's Bazaar* among others. She built her brand from the ground up, after walking away from a corporate career to follow her heart.

It was from this personal journey that she was driven to write her first book "*Passion, Fashion & Heart*", which quickly became an Amazon Best Seller.

Christina knew it was her purpose to inspire and empower women through her passion for fashion. With a desire to have them feel beautiful inside and out and live a life they love, but most importantly themselves.

Dedication

This guide is dedicated to sisterhood and created with love for all you gorgeous women out there, all ages and sizes wherever you are in the world. Whatever your role in life may be, I want to make fashion easy and fun.

This is for YOU everything you need to know on how to dress, style, shop, and love your bodyshape. You my friends deserve to feel fantastic inside and out, so let's make it happen together!

With much love,

I created this fashion guide for all the fabulous and amazing women out there, from around the globe and all walks of life. We are all created with a touch of magic, with unique and beautiful shapes that were made just for us. They have our names on them, nobody else's and intended for you and me.

Let's learn how to highlight them in the right places, embrace them, work with them, and most importantly – love them. They are waiting for you to adorn them in the right way, bring out their fabulous parts. The inner goddess, the rock star chic, whoever may be hiding in there and let her rule. Wear that crown my friend!

Women are beautiful and individual, so it's important that you wear the right clothes for your body. Do you need to drape, accentuate or elongate and how? What do you need to do? Yes, it can be overwhelming but don't worry we've got this!

You can obtain the most beautiful clothes in the world, but if you don't know what to wear and how to wear them, you are not doing your body justice. Sometimes we may not love what we see in the mirror, we know we can look and feel better but don't quite know how. That is why I was inspired to write my book and create this guide, because we all deserve to feel beautiful inside and out.

You will get detailed information on each body shape. What clothes should be gracing your body, and which should never touch it. You'll learn when to say, "Yes! I want that in every color!". When to say, "No!' and throw it wildly out of your closet, and when to say "Never Ever!" and pass it on. There are also blank pages to jot down any notes.

I have focused on the five body shapes, yes you may differ slightly and be a pear with a big bust, or an hourglass with a small bust. Overall working with the five simple body shapes will give you a very good idea on what is yours. To the point you will know what to wear and what not to wear. I don't want you to get caught up with too many shapes, just choose the closest to yours and go from there. I want this to be an easy fun process, not a confusing stressful one!

I have also included other goodies, styling and shopping tips, layering, choosing the right jeans for your shaped tush, bras and shape-wear and all you need to know about color and skin tones.

This is created with the style and body shape chapters from my book, "Passion, Fashion & Heart". I wanted you to have a quick and easy way of pulling up everything you need to know, on the go, wherever you are. I know how hectic a modern woman's lifestyle can be and time is everything especially if you also have the title of mother.

It can be hard to remember what you should be looking for in the exciting throws of shopping, especially if you see something you fall madly in love with. You can now effortlessly double check if the style is right for your shape. Then and there. Boom!

This pocket rocket book is not only super cute, but practical and a great size to pop in your pretty little handbag. It could also save you money and future fashion disasters. No more refunds, exchanges and wrong impulse buys that sit in the depths of your closet.

You will see the body shapes also have names – Emma, Mandy, Jayne, Alice and Georgie. These are the five ladies that I followed and wrote about in my book. Sharing their personal and confronting stories about how they came, learnt to love and dress their own body shapes, but most importantly themselves, and they totally conquered!

Right you fabulous ladies... let's get started!

Christina x

Testmonials

"Christina's unpretentious ideas about body type and color palette that inspire the modern-woman to look her best, whether casual or fancy, anywhere, anytime. Because when you finally get it right about what looks best on you, you're confident and there's just no stopping you, is there.

Tami Smith
Communications Coach & special events presenter
LA. California

"The great tips on fashion and styling are so helpful and inspiring"

Sarah Anna
Fashion Designer. Influencer. TV Host, Germany

"This book is amazing and I love it! Great easy tips on styling. A must read!"

Monica Villar
Founder of Amanda Chic. Editor. Influences fashion, travel & lifestyle blogger Spain.

"One of the most informative styling boohs I have come across to date. Need some styling advice on topics such as body shapes, color palettes and shin tones? This book covers all the basics. You want to know how to look and feel amazing? Then you definitely need this booh in your life"

Saffron Edwards
First Class Fashion Stylist
Wales. UK

"Christina shows you how to look and feel fabulous whatever shape you have. "This is not just about fashion, it is about self-esteem and acceptance, and learning to love yourself"

Patrik Simpson
TV personality
"Gown and out in Beverly Hills". LA.

"Packed fabulously full of great advice that comes from the heart. Her love for wanting to mahe other women feel good, her dedication and absolute love for what she does leaves you wanting more."

Pol' Atteu
Celebrity Fashion designer. TV personality "Gown and out in Beverly Hills". LA

"A definitive how to guide on fashion and making the most out of your bodyshape".

Leigh O'Connor
Writer AGF Magazine. Australia

"The style guide is very clear, useful and full of handy tips"

Maddy McGlynn
Editor Canada

Dressing myself everyday was a chore, with trying on several outfits or combinations all having the same result: where I looked just "drab" It got to the point where I wouldn't even fight it anymore, I knew that whatever I chose from my closet was just going to make me look "ordinary", but Christina's book changed all that I'm 50 and now feel like I'm in my 20's!

The clothes I choose make me look and feel fabulous. I was not dressing for my body shape and accentuating my less desirable features.

Choosing clothes and dressing my body shape based on Christina's advice has given me a "WOW" factor. I have never received so many compliments on the way I look in such a short period of time.

The other mothers ask if I've had work done and what my diet is. My diet was Christina's book! If you are not getting compliments on the way you look… Christina's book is food for thought!

Maria Sullivan
Mother of three. Award winning CEO of International Business Connect Named top 20 Influencer of Women in IT United States.

Contents

Emma The Pear
Page 1

Jayne The Strawberry
Page 9

Mandy The Apple
Page 17

Alice The Hourglass
Page 25

Georgie The Pillar
Page 33

Bra's & Shapewear
Page 41

Colors & Skin Tones
Page 53

Style Fact File
Page 73

Shopping Tips
Page 89

Christina's Special Message
Page 99

The Pear – The Emma

It's always all about finding balance between your top and your bottom. For the Pear, just keep the focus on your lovely slim top and the rest will naturally follow.

The key to remember here is thighs.

The Pear may look like she has got wide hips but actually, it's the thighs where the width is. Basically, your lower body is wider than your upper body.

To create that body balance, you will need to take emphasis away from the thighs/hips and draw it to the top half of your body. We want to add volume to the shoulders and upper body. Your bottom is rounded and your waist is well defined.

You can do this easily by just choosing tops with the right style and shape and also picking bold designs and colors. You can have fun with the upper deck so go all out and get creative and find your own personal style.

Now, the area below the knee we really need to draw outward and elongate that central part. Choose visually interesting hemlines that are wider, this will balance out the hip/thighs area, also making it appear slimmer. The hi-low styles would be great.

Usually Pear shaped ladies have narrower shoulders and a smaller bust in comparison to the waist and lower half of the body. Of course, you will need a great fitting bra, that goes without saying.

Fabulous parts of the pear – your shoulders and torso.

Dressing the pear

No you can't – lower deck

- Avoid short, tight skirts and pencil skirts, as they emphasize those problematic areas along the hips and thighs.
- Avoid clingy materials because these will just define the hips and thighs we would like to minimize.
- Bright colors on the lower half draw the eye, and you want to draw the eye somewhere else. Go with darker colors on the lower half and bring interest to the upper half to give balance.
- A skinny jean is going to hug every inch of your legs and the issue here is that it's hugging every inch of your legs! These are the least flattering for your shape.
- Avoid light, pale and "washed look" jeans. Especially ones that have the worn look around the upper leg and body section, as this will draw the eye to this area.
- Stay away from bias cut skirts. They are designed to highlight the hips by draping themselves all over them. This may be wonderful for another shape but for you they're going to be highlighting your thighs. We don't want that.

Yes you can – lower deck

- Wear darker colors on your lower body. This gives a slimming effect and isn't distracting.
- Remember not to highlight your lower half, in fact really minimize here. Keep things super simple.
- Hems of pants, skirts, and dresses need to be wider to balance out the hip / thighs.
- A-line skirts (longer length) and wrap dresses are great for Pears because they skim over those lovely curves without making them look unshapely. The clever weapon in working with your lower half is the wider leg pants.
- The straighter leg with a flare at the bottom half to create a full volume all the way to the bottom. These wider leg styles are your best option. It confuses the eye into thinking your thighs are thinner than they are and your legs are longer. Pants and jeans that are equal width or a little wider in the calf and ankle area, draw the eye away from the hip / thigh area.
- Pants and skirts that are flat-fronted or softly pleated will emphasize your smaller waist area.
- Visually interesting hemlines for skirts, pants and dresses are great, as this balances out the hip/thighs area making it appear slimmer.
- Wear the hi-low styles, these are also super comfy as well as looking fab on your shape.
- Tulip style would also work well.
- For jeans, choose darker shades of denim that will give more of a slimming effect.

- For pants and skirts wear darker blues, dark grays, blacks, browns and olive green – these are the best shades to work with. They will also go with most shirt colors.
- Jeans with fading below the knee can also work well for you. Again bringing the eye downwards.

Yes you can – upper deck

- Be fun and get creative with the tops you wear. You will find that it is difficult to go wrong when choosing tops with color, detail, and pattern that will draw the eyes upwards. So have fun, especially with the neckline, which is perfect for that added detail.
- Think embellishments with beading and collars. Scarves are great. Remember we want to highlight this upper half.
- Choose wider necklines, like boat neck, squared, sweetheart, V-neck or cowl to show off the neckline and shoulders. Show us the skin.
- Try some ruffles on the top (yes you are allowed). Also layering works.
- Jackets should be just above the waist and coats follow the same rule as the tops, the length of the coat can be either waist length or three quarter, this length will nicely cover your less than flattering areas.
- A belted coat with a structured skirt will emphasize your small waist, add volume to your upper half and deceive the eye about the shape of your lower half.

- Try something with some detail on the shoulder, this can work well here. Also, a pattern or detail to the bust and cuff area of the coat is great. Double breasted coats will give a fab balanced look. They also have such an elegant look about them.
- Add a shrug or cropped jacket to that strapless dress to attract more attention to your upper half. Because it finishes just under your breasts, it highlights the bust as well, again making your upper half look wider.
- Tops should be fitted and not baggy and should finish at the top of your waist to emphasize your well-defined waist.
- Invest in a good push-up bra to give yourself the oomph you need to show off that fabulous shape.
- For you Pears, the key when it comes to buying that perfect dress is to draw all the attention up top, you should show off your lovely arms, back, and bust.
- Strapless dresses with a generous skirt will look great on you, if you don't feel daring enough to show all that skin try a halter neck. They are fitted up top, which will show off your waist. Dresses with spaghetti straps will give your shoulders a slightly broader appearance and help balance you out.

No you can't – upper deck

- Avoid tops and jackets that end at your bottom because these draw the eye to your middle section, which we do not want to highlight.
- Don't wear baggy square tops that don't define your waist.
- Don't wear high necklines that cover up all the chest area.

Shoes

- Pointy toed shoes elongate the legs, so go for them.
- A straight boot will hide wider calves, and can look stylish and classy with almost anything.
- A thin stiletto and delicate heel is not a good idea as it will make them look bigger again. This doesn't mean you need to give up heels, just go for a chunkier one.
- Heels with an ankle strap just cut the leg off, making it look shorter, the straps have the same effect as the stiletto. There are plenty of options out there in your best suited style so don't worry about that.
- Wear small wedge shoes for great balance to your frame.

Bags

- Choose a short shoulder bag that finishes and sits above your waist, no lower. You don't want anything sitting around the though area.

Swimwear

- For this shape, it is about focusing upstairs, drawing attention away from the thigh/hip area to create visual balance for your body. Showing your best parts!
- If you are choosing a two-piece, opt for skirtinis and tankinis. With the tops, embrace it and go for detail, visual interest, prints, patterns, colors and embellishments.
- You are one of the body shapes that can go all out here!
- Look for a simple skirted bottom that falls just below the widest part of your thigh.
- Avoid wearing a boy short or thick-banded bottom, this is not flattering for you.
- Avoid colorful sarongs and bikini bottoms that draw your eyes to the thigh/hip area.
- Go for a lower cut bikini bottom. Avoid the high cut bottoms, as exposing too much skin around the lower area doesn't work for you. Basically for the bottoms, it is the opposite to the top! Keep it simple, keep it dark with no embellishments, details, ties, ruffles etc. If it looks interesting – don't go there!
- If you are choosing a one piece, look for the block dark bottom, with a patterned/colored and fun top. Again simple downstairs and exciting upstairs!
- A plunging neckline, triangle, sweetheart and halter styles are all fabulous for you.
- Think eye-catching. Accentuating the bust is visually creating a slimming lower half.

The Strawberry – The Jayne

This body shape has a generous bust, wide shoulders, longer legs and narrow waist and hips. Basically, your lower half is smaller than your top half. Your shoulders are wider than your hips. These are the defining features of the Strawberry. Also known as the Inverted Triangle or the Lollipop.

Balancing the figure and de-emphasizing the broadness up top are the keys to this shape. We need to accentuate the lower body while gently softening the upper body, especially the shoulders.

This means you need to subtly broaden the hips and also accentuate the waist, to take away the look that can be too top heavy. You need to look at styles that even out your figure a little, to make the proportions balanced. A great fitting bra that sits and lifts correctly is a must. The key for this shape is really to create visual balance.

Fabulous parts – your legs!

Dressing the strawberry

No you can't – upper deck

- Polo neck or high neck tops/sweaters, no boat neck styles.
- No details and added volume on your shoulders, for example, no puff sleeves, gathers or shoulder pads.
- No oversized collars or lapels.
- Stay away from bold patterns on top, it will just make you look wider. No horizontal stripes.

- Chunky knitwear will make you look top heavy, so steer clear of it. Just think – no bulk upstairs.
- Don't wear anything that hangs loosely from the bust. Shift dresses are not flattering to your shape. Don't wear styles that hide your silhouette.

No you can't – lower deck

- Avoid flat fronts
- Stay away from a cut that is too tight or skinny, as you are in danger of looking too top heavy. No tapered in skirts.
- Also don't wear very wide leg pants as they can make your legs look like sticks and unnaturally thin. Plus you hide those fabulous legs. The more bootleg style that flares our gradually toward the hemline, the best for your shape.
- High waist pants and skirts do not work well.

Yes you can – top deck

- Scoop neck tops – along with deep V-necks, are an essential part of your wardrobe, preferably in knit fabrics.
- Square and sweetheart necklines also work. Basically, we are after some expanse up top. Nothing closed up. Show us some skin.
- Wear tops that are nipped in at the waist, with banding or wrap style tops and finish just on the hip bone. A little flare at the bottom of tops and jackets is great, adds curve to the hips.

- With the said necklines it will open up and take the focus off your shoulders whilst the rest of the top will hug your waist and emphasize your curves. What is not to love?
- A wide neck jacket or coat is great, again we are opening up that neckline. It is a must for anyone with a big bust. So make sure the jacket or coat has wide lapels.
- Buttons underneath the breasts, particularly two buttons nip it in beautifully as you're so slender everywhere else. This will accommodate your bust whilst drawing attention to your small waist. Wear jackets open to create a vertical line.
- Wear darker colors on top and textures that have a light look to them, to soften the shoulder line.
- Wear crop jackets where the hemline sits on the waist. The horizontal line will further emphasize the waist.
- Balloon sleeves help create curves in areas that have less.
- Peplum styles are fab as they create an illusion of hips, details on the hips work well. Balancing out that top half and focusing on the waist.
- Wear belts, they are wonderful for accentuation the waist.

Yes you can – lower deck

- Wear bright colors
- Wear full skirts
- Gathered dresses are perfect for your shape.

- The most subtle weapon is that waist. It is fabulous so work with it.
- You can wear belts or dresses with defined waistbands to draw attention to that small waist with your torso curving into it from above and below.
- Wear a dress that opens up your chest so your bust doesn't look trapped and suffocated, it will again emphasize your waist. Other than your bust you don't have a lot of curves going on.
- Draped fabrics are really good as they will adore and hug your hips, creating curves.
- An alternative is to cinch in the waist using the buttons of a jacket and if you are brave enough you can even go for a crop top and bare the midriff.
- The perfect skirt for this body shape is an A-line as it flares out from your hips. Creating an overall balance.
- Fluted/Tulip skirts are a great subtle means of creating a curve. Your slender legs will still look great but there is now some bulk below the waist.
- Pleated skirts also add volume below the waist in a gorgeous way. The pleats will help the skirt to move and fall in a manner that is chic and sophisticated.
- Bold prints and textures can also be effectively used to draw the eye down, you can also wear plain black on top as a slimming contrast. Horizontal stripes will make the lower half look wider.

- Wear trousers / pants that are mid to low rise and if you can with some detail at the hip. Pockets and embellishments at the front for added bulk (in a good way). Flap pockets work well.
- Pockets at the back can create an illusion of more volume on your butt. Even though this may seem outrageous to other shapes of talking about adding volume. For the Strawberry though, it balances out your body.
- Boot leg jeans and trousers with a slight flare below the knee, subtly create curves. The hems of the trousers will balance out your upper body and you'll look impossibly tall and curvaceous. Oh yes, we love that!
- Jeans with whiskering at the hips are great.

Shoes

- Slim / stiletto heels are fab for your shape – your calves are slender so a thin heel looks perfectly in proportion. Go bold and eye-catching with your footwear.
- Slim/stiletto heels are fab for your shape – your calves are slender so a thin heel looks perfectly in proportion. Go bold and eye-catching with your footwear.

Bags

- Choose a clutch or a shoulder bag that finishes at the waist.

Swimwear

- Swimwear styles for your shape are all about drawing the eye down to your waist and hips to give visual balance. Do this by wearing fuller shapes with patterns or a skirt at the bottom and higher cut with ties at the sides. Gathered/ruched sides are classy and work well to bring focus to your fab legs! Think visual interest on the bottoms, patterns and color!

- A great way to define your waist with a two piece is going for a midriff coverage. Again that ruching around the middle area just brings out your waist. Tankinis are great for support and to create balance as well.

- For the top, in both one and two pieces, opt for an underwire or molded cups for support and a great look, thicker straps are also a good idea. If you go for a string bikini top, you can adjust the triangle to fit nicely over your ladies, so then there is good balance.

- If you are choosing the triangle top, be careful it is simple with not too much interest, so we bring the eye down. Halter works well. Avoid styles that give a wide shoulder and bust visual, like strapless/bandeau.

- Another option is the lovely sweetheart neckline, it often offers thicker straps too, showing off the ladies without obvious focus in a sophisticated way!

- You can wear one or two pieces, depending on what you are most comfortable with. The one piece suits are actually a fab option for your shape too if you go for a high cut leg which is an easy way to balance the top half. Go for waistline detail/interest, patterns that are focused centre stage to give off a wow waist!

The Apple – The Mandy

This body shape of the Apple is best described as round. Your waist is not defined and is your widest part. You don't have to have a very large tummy to be an Apple, it just means that is where your extra weight resides. You have a flatter bottom and your shoulders tend to be broad. You have thinner arms and legs and your hips are narrower than your bust.

With Apples you are likely to have great boobs, so make use of them, keep the focus up top, rather than down below. Showing off your bust not only emphasizes one of your greatest features, it will draws the eye away from the middle area.

Tummy's impact on the rest of your frame. The first step for apples is to get a great fitting bra. You need clear definition between your bust and your tummy. This will make all the difference.

Fabulous parts of the Apple – your boobs.

Dressing an Apple

No you can't – upper deck

- High necklines, no tops that cover your chest area, we need to open that up and show expanse.
- Large shapeless tops that don't show any waist. Keep it more straight lined and very slightly fitted, just nothing that hangs square.
- Heavy bulky jackets that just add volume to your upper half. No lapels, double breasted coats and jackets. Don't wear belts, big or small. They will not flatter you.

- Stay away from detail, added bulk, excessive fabric, tiers, gathers, ruching around the bust, waist and tummy areas. Keep any detail above the bust line and below the hip line. In between those lines keep it plain and simple so as to not draw the eye to that area.
- Don't wear sleeves that finish near your bust line

Yes you can – upper deck

- Flattering draping/flowing fabrics yet still with some shape, not ones that hang square. Straighter lines.
- Tops that are tight under the bust, that highlight your body at the slimmest part, which is often just under the breast line and length that finishes just below the hip line.
- Wear V-neck tops and basically any tops that open you up at the chest area.
- Shirts also look best when they are fitted just underneath the bust and then flare out.
- Also try to get the V-shape happening with your shirts. Again we want to see skin up top.
- Dresses should have their waistline just below the bust. Baby doll style is great. A-line dresses also elongate your body and draw attention upstairs.
- Patterns and prints look fab on an Apple shape body as they latter and camouflage all at once. Do not wear a completely different band of print or pattern just around the tummy area or again you will look straight there even if it is still patterned.

- Straight lapel jacket or cardigan with V-shape at top – we want to confuse and deceive the eye. Try wearing a straight lapel jacket or cardigan open over a fitted shirt. This creates three distinct portions through the middle of your body, each long and slim. Elongating your frame.
- A straight cut coat that ends just above the knee will create a nice long silhouette.
- Tops with detail above the bust line that draws attention there and confuses the eye.

Yes you can – lower deck

- Think plain and simple for the tummy and hip area.
- Get trousers that have zippers at the side to avoid adding extra bulk on the front. We don't want any clinging to the tummy or thighs. Avoid pleats if you can but if there are pleats they must be below the belly line.
- Choose jeans that have a great cut and are either straight or flared.
- Choose skirts that have their zippers at the side. Structured pencil skirts work well, but keep them at knee length. Don't go above knee length.
- Make sure that any pleats of skirts or dresses start below the belly to avoid adding extra volume.

No you can't – lower deck

- High waisted trousers and pants with chunky zips and pockets at the front.
- No waistbands.
- Keep your skirt/dress length knee or below.
- No detail and volume around tummy and hip area. Once again, plain and simple is the key.
- No pleats in the tummy area.
- No belts on waist or hip, big or small.

Shoes

- A small shaped wedge is a great heel for you – it works well in showing off your slim ankles, while giving you good support at the same time. It also avoids any unnecessary contrast between the size of your upper body and the slenderness of your lower legs. Avoid kitten and petite heels. Boots also don't flatter.
- For evening wear, choose a higher and sexier heel in the same wedge shape.
- A small shaped wedge heel is great for you – it works well in showing off your slim ankles, while giving you good support at the same time. It also avoids any unnecessary contrast between the size of your upper body and the slenderness of your lower legs. Avoid kitten and petite heels. Boots also don't flatter.
- For evening wear, choose a higher and sexier heel in the same wedge shape.

Bags

- Choose a clutch or a longer shoulder bag as you don't want n sitting and finishing right on the waist area. It just adds bulk.

Swimwear

- This shape needs to highlight those fabulous legs and draw attention away from the middle area. By picking the right pieces that focus upstairs, it will elongate your body. Remember there are also some great swimwear options now with the tummy shapers and hidden control panels, and you are the only one that knows! Great for that feeling of a little extra support.
- The classic one piece is perfect if you're looking for more coverage over your tummy. If opting for this, go for high cut legs showing them off!
- Look for the side ruching detail at the waist, this absolutely flatters your shape and minimizes your tummy. The gathered fabric hides wee bulges and defines your waist. For you it is a miracle worker! The wrap style in the middle section also works really well with the crossover fabric.
- Go for dark solid colours for slimming, or patterned as this confuses the eye and flatters. The sweetheart, halter or plunging necklines are great. Why? It draws us up to the fabulous top! Have fun, go for detail, visual interest and pattern.

- If opting for a two piece, go for a patterned style taking the eye up to the top and down to the bottom, avoiding the tummy area. Again you want a higher cut bottom to lengthen the leg, creating a lovely lean silhouette.
- If your weight is more in the lower tummy, try the retro high waisted bottoms. These go up and over, smoothing out the tummy and covering the abdomen. The ruching in this style would be fab too.

The Hourglass – The Alice

The Hourglass shape is all about those womanly curves.

Your bust and hips are well balanced and you have a beautifully defined waist.

Your upper body is proportionate in length to your legs, which are shapely. Your waist is small in comparison to your hips and bust. The key to dressing an Hourglass body type is to proportionally dress the top and bottom of your body while accentuating your waist.

All an hourglass woman needs to do is dress in clothes that follow the curves of her body shape, it's simply a case of realizing you have nothing to hide and accentuating everything you have.

Fabulous part of the hourglass – your super little waist.

Let me now tell you, this is my body shape so all you hourglass women out there… I get ya ladies… I feel ya! Years ago I really struggled with trying to figure out my shape, what I could wear and what I couldn't. Realizing that some of the things I loved to wear, I really shouldn't be wearing and vise versa.

That was the hardest but once I just embraced my shape and came to the conclusion that this is my body. There is no swapping, exchanging, getting a refund, this is me and this is what I have. I will be grateful for my body. So I will learn all about it and wear the best possible clothes that flatter me and make me feel unstoppable. I did, and now I love m shape and it loves me because I adorn it with all the clothes it loves to wear.

It did take me some time to get my head around being able to wear figure hugging clothing. To me it felt very, "look at me, look at me." Now I understand that it's ok as its best for my shape, of course also along with other styles. One of my all-time faves is the fit and flare dress. Now let's get into it and find out what we should and shouldn't be wearing if we are an Hourglass body shape.

Dressing the hourglass body

No you can't – lower deck

- Avoid low-rise pants, since these may make your hips look wider and your legs look shorter. Mid-rise and high-rise cuts elongate the leg.
- Skinny leg jeans should also be avoided.
- Square box shape hanging dresses, or anything else that hides your waist. Baggy clothes will completely hide your figure not to mention make you look wide. You have a fabulous waist and shape so let's see it.
- Pants and skirts that have too much detail going on. No chunky stuff, embellishments, and pleats. Anything that will draw the eye to your hips making them look bigger.

Yes you can – lower deck

- A pencil skirt is made for an Hourglass. The way it holds itself around your curves is perfect to show off your feminine shape, you have the body to carry it off. Wear it with a fitted top to show off your tiny waist and maintain balance.

- Flared and skater style skirts look great on your curves.
- Stick with mid-rise or high-rise pants, these cuts elongate the leg. Styles with wide waist-bands and yokes are especially flattering.
- Boot-cut styles. The slight flare keeps the bottom portion of your leg in balance with your wide hips. This also creates a longer, slimmer appearance for your legs.
- Fitted dresses that elongate the waist, choose an open neckline to open up your chest and minimize your bust. From there look for a dress that fits your shape, nipping in at the waist at a lower point. Fit and flare style works with your shape whilst making your waist look longer and consequently the whole shape taller and slimmer.

No you can't – upper deck

- Avoid straight and boxy style jackets as they do not show your waist and will make you appear heavier.
- Baggy sleeves
- Flouncy blouses
- Anything lose fitting and with no shape is to be avoided.

- High necklines are a big no. A polo neck will make your boobs look disproportionately large. We want balance.
- No ruffles, pleats or chunky stuff going on up there. It will just draw attention there.
- No double breasted jackets and coats, all that does is add bulk.

Yes you can – upper deck

- Go for jackets that follow your body line and draw in toward the waist. Short jackets that stop just above your hips accentuate your curves in a flattering way and makes you look taller and slimmer. Look for form-fitting and belted jackets. Also, single buttoned jackets as they don't add bulk.
- Cardigans/tops with plunging necks, V-necklines, scoops, and sweethearts are a must. Wrap style works well too.
- Look for tops that will accentuate your waist and maintain the balanced look of your figure:
- Belted tops
- Tops with banding or nipping at the waist § Form-fitting tops
- Tops that finish just below the hip line, this makes you look taller and slimmer
- Wrap-style tops.
- Tailored shirts and jackets.

- Fitted dresses that nip in at the waist showing it off. Wrap and fit and flare styles are fabulous.

Shoes

- Do not wear chunky shoes.
- A slimmer to medium heel works well.
- Wear a heel that's in keeping with your frame. Look for rounded toes or peep toes. Avoid pointy shoes.
- Wear shoes with a thin to medium heel. No chunky shoes. A peep toe or rounded toe work really well, just not pointed.

Bags

- Choose a clutch or a short shoulder bag that finishes and sits at the waist.

Swimwear

- In the swimwear department you definitely have more options and can pick and choose different silhouettes. It's all about the curves and they are gorgeous, so go for it!
- Your body shape looks great in a classic bikini with a bra style top. Avoid the top heavy look with any high neck styles (for one and two pieces). Take the time and focus on the top, making sure you have the coverage you want, the underwire is fab support and to hold the ladies in, to have them looking their best! Retro styles are a winner

- A classic bikini bottom looks great but avoid the short briefs that cut low at the hips, this isn't flattering for you and instantly shortens, halter, scoop or V necks look awesome. Cutouts, interest, color blocking at the waist is flattering, as they accentuate it, drawing the eye there to create that visual balance.
- For colors in pieces, go for matching instead of mixing. Tops and bottoms that are the same colors or patterns will give you balance, mixing pieces can give an out of proportion look.

The Pillar – The Georgie

Pillars are generally taller and have shoulders the same size as their hips, slim waists and long legs. Also known as the Column. They don't have broad shoulders but their busts are the same width as their slender hips. They don't have much in the way of a waist, tummy or bottom.

The Pillar body shape is very much straight up and down. The key to making Pillars look their best is to try to introduce a little shape and emphasize or create curves.

Pillars are really to be envied, as very easily, they can look super. It doesn't take much at all. You need to create the illusion of hips, bust and end of waist areas.

The real issue is that your curves can disappear by simply being stretched out over your long frame. The best way to bring those curves back is to use blocks of color. In that way, you can make gorgeous use of your long legs, arms, and body without ending up looking like a Pillar. Avoid anything that is shapeless and hangs straight up and down.

Key for your shape – add curve. Just define and highlight that waist and you are good to go.

Fabulous part of the Pillar – gorgeous tall lean frame.

Dressing the Pillar

No you can't – upper deck

- Anything shapeless, particularly long coats, jackets, and dresses. We don't want any baggy styles that just hang from the shoulders. No double breasted jackets.
- Straight dresses in one block color does not flatter your shape, a Pillar is straight up and down, so wearing a dress that's straight up and down just emphasizes that exact fact. You will have no shape at all. Not good.
- Cropped tops are not a good style for you, your body is long and so are your legs. So all it will do is shorten the length of your body, which is then added onto the length of your legs, resulting in them looking out of proportion.
- Don't wear boxy jackets – they will emphasize the straight up and down of your torso.
- Long straight fitted sleeves don't work well. We want to create a roundness.
- Avoid square necklines on tops and dresses. No bulky and heavy textures.

Yes you can – upper deck

- Round necklines are great for you, as it softens the straight Pillar lines. A round neck line or a V-neck adds a touch of elegance.
- You look great in any length sleeve, sleeveless tops also show off your lean arms. The fluted and flared sleeve is the best option to add a little shape and avoid the straight up and down look.

- You have the perfect shape for a shirt but the best option is going to be something that breaks up the long expanse of your torso. Look for something that is textured and gathered at the waist to give you some curve.
- Angular shapes are great for the Pillar, especially if every line points to the middle.
- Strategically placed lapels or pockets, flared or wod sleeves, pointed hemline, fitted waist with single button fastening, or belts, do that exact thing. The idea of the single button jacket is to breakup your torso, which the single button does, kind of like drawing a target there and defining it.
- Belted three-quarter length coat with hip pockets are perfect, as the length shows off the legs, the belt and hip pockets add curves and defines the waist.
- Wear accessories and keep them big, bold and as a statement to the outfit to add shape. Avoid anything too thin or long.
- Add shape with detail, a belt or peplum style is fab as it will give you great curves.
- Use layering to shorten the longer top half of your body.

No you can't – lower deck

- Don't wear a dropped waist, as it makes the legs shorter but also makes the torso look unnaturally long.
- Avoid full length block colors.

- Stay away from anything shapeless that just hangs straight up and down.
- Avoid long straight fitted lines in pants and dresses. We want roundness.

Yes you can – lower deck

- Highlight that waist. Accentuate it, nip it in.
- Wear high or low waisted styles, which veer to your waist.
- Highlight your hips and bottom by using pockets and pleats. Remember we want to create visual curves.
- Although you can wear practically any shaped pant the best idea is to go for one with a slight flare to add a little curve to your body. Break up and show off those super long Pillar legs. Cropped style also works well for you.
- An A-line skirt does the same job as a slight flare on the trousers, drawing attention to their curves. Choose a gently flaring A-line to give your lower half some shape. Mix up colors and patterns and have fun working out your own personal style.
- A bias cut dress, usually in chiffon, clings to every curve. The Pillar is perfectly shaped to pull it off.
- Choose something with floaty sleeves that will utilize your long arms. This example works so well because it will draw attention to your tiny waist, and the different blocks of color will further break up your long body.
- Fitted angular style dresses look great.

Shoes

- The heel should not be too thin, not too thick, just perfectly balanced. What matters is that you feel comfortable and supported. Other than that, you can get away with any style shoe. Flats are as good as heels for you.
- You can wear many different shoes but keep total balance, so don't wear too chunky a heels, and don't wear too thin a heel. Keep it in the middle for perfect balance for your frame.

Bags

- When adding a bag you can pretty much choose, you are trying to create curves so I would suggest a bag finishing at the waist area to accentuate the waist and break up the body.

Swimwear

- For this shape is it your goal to create curves! We want styles that show off your gorgeous frame and expose some skin. By doing this it is creating the illusion of a beautiful curvy figure.
- If opting for a one piece this can look super classy, as it throws a visual of a smaller waist. Cut-outs on the side and monokinis are fabulous for your shape, as it draws attention to the waist creating a shapely figure top and bottom.

- To give the illusion of a lovely shape around the hips and bottom, wear a higher cut leg. Basically the less coverage for your shape the better! The retro inspired one pieces can work really well for you too, especially with ruching which creates once again a curvy visual-being the goal!
- Padding in the bust to add that extra oomph or bold bright patterns and horizontal stripes are all great if you are lacking a little upstairs. The halter neck style also adds some extra cleavage.
- If you are going for a two piece go all out and have some fun! Do ruffles, bold prints/patterns, embellishments for the top and the bottom, this creates the illusion of fabulous curves upstairs and downstairs.
- The side tie bikini bottoms are great as they enhance curves and you can adjust exactly to your size. The smaller the bikini bottom, the curvier the butt looks..which is what you want!

Bra's & Shapewear

All you need to know on what lies beneath...!

Regardless of your size, shape wear can be the icing on that beautiful, rich triple decker, delicious decadent chocolate cake. Adorned with a gorgeous dark red shiny cherry. It smooths and tightens and enhances to reveal a fabulous silhouette. The right fitting bra and any shape wear is only going to give you that beautiful cherry sitting pert and pretty at the very top. So why not at least try it? Let's talk about... What lies beneath...

Firstly, let's kick off with the bra. Finding the right bra size can really be a mission for many women; it can be overwhelming and in the end, you just deal with it and wear what you have in the drawer. It is estimated that about eighty percent of women wear the wrong size bra.

That's a lot of uncomfortable women out there, right? It is not a great thing for your ladies, nor is it healthy.

We need to look after these ladies and a bra that is too tight, is frankly my dear...not a good thing. We will learn together how to measure your bust and sort this out once and for all. Let's get you feeling comfortable and looking great with a perfect profile upstairs. We have enough going on in our busy lives, and we don't need to be wriggling, squirming, adjusting and pulling at ourselves, throughout the day. I mean, why the torture? Exactly.

We look after our skin, don't we? We cleanse and tone and moisturize, trying all sorts of creams and potions. Some of us go to spas, get massages, treatments, vitamins, the works. Yet giving our ladies the attention they deserve, to keep them well and healthy in their house, seems to just get thrown in the "too hard basket". Actually, once we do get it right, that's it, all done.

When we know our correct bra size and type, then we know it, forever. It's not like our bra size changes every week or two and we need to keep getting a refit.

They are far less work than any other part of our body. So this is really a one off effort and we have those ladies settled and comfortable. Do it once and do it right.

Discover your band size

A bra's band should fit snug, its cups should contain the breast tissue, the straps should assist the bra, not support the breasts. 90% of bra support is in the band. It's your suspension bridge, your foundation, your way to a perfect fit. The band is literally your bra's base and is built to support your breasts. If it's not secure, you're not secure. It should feel comfortably snug, and sit perfectly level around, front to back.

If it rides up your back, it's too big. If your straps are falling, it's too loose. It must be snug. A good rule of thumb is, if you can use two fingers to comfortably skim the inside of the band, it's correct. If there's slack in the back, your bra may be worn or you may need a smaller band.

Have someone measure around your chest with a tape measure, just under your breasts, and around the back. Make sure the tape measure rests flat on the skin and goes straight across your back.

The "old" advice has been to add five inches to this measurement and then that is your band size (also called chest size). HOWEVER, adding only two to three inches (instead of 5) works better for most women. You can even try not adding to the measurement you get, and just using that as your band size.

This is because the band is elasticated and because the bra needs to fit snugly so it can provide about 80-90% of the support for the ladies – and then the straps (shoulder) only carry about 10-20% of the load. Oh dear, it really sounds a bit like a dump truck, doesn't it?

Finding your ladies perfect cup size

What's the gore?

The gore is the center panel of an underwire bra. The part of the bra that connects the cups in the front, between the breasts. Not all bras have the same type or size gore, and some styles don't have this part at all. But if your bra has an underwire, then the gore will always be the part that's "center front" and it should typically lie flat against your body.

Your underwire should fit firmly against your chest without any gaping. Assuming your straps are properly adjusted, you'll know you've found the right band fit when you can lift your arms over your head without the underwire rising up. The cup should hold your entire breast without the dreaded quadra-boob.

Have someone measure you. The measuring tape goes on top of the fullest part of your breasts. Record this number, and find the difference between that, and the band-size number. The difference tells you the correct cup size as follows.

While this is useful for determining the cup size, bear in mind that 34A cup does NOT have the same exact volume as 36A or 38A. Similarly, 30D does not have the same volume as 36D (30D is a much smaller cup than 36D). So, if you try on a 36B bra and the cup size fits but the band is too loose so that you decide to go to down in band size to 34, you may actually need 34C cup size so as to have about the same volume in the bra cup.

Even with a measurement, it is better to try on different bras and find out experimentally which one fits.

Just remember to go by the fit, not by the numbers. You have to try the bra on.

If it fits right, that's your bra size, even if the tape measure told you differently. To avoid breasts side walling instead of going straight forward… look for a bra with a four part cup. The additional seam on the side, known as a "side sling", is great for helping guide your ladies forward.

What styles best flatter your ladies?

The shape of your breasts and torso are unique. Depending on your particular proportions, certain styles will look better on you than others.

Your bra will look better if it flatters the overall proportion of your torso. Ideally, your shoulders should look about the same width as your hips.

If your shoulders are broad, try to find bras with narrower straps, and a shape that plunges more in the middle.

If your shoulders are narrow, look for bras that create a more distinct horizontal line across your torso. If your torso is short, a bra that plunges more in the middle can elongate your torso. Think about the shape of your breasts. There are so many types of breast shapes and sizes.

How to tell if the ladies are sitting perfectly — are they where they should be?

If you are wearing an underwire bra, the wire that comes up between the breasts should lay flat (or as close as possible) to your breast bone.

If you are wearing a bra with no underwire, you should have two separate breasts, not just "one big boob"... not a good look at all.

If the bra is a soft cup bra, you shouldn't have any extra, loose fabric. If the bra is a molded cup you shouldn't have any extra room in the cup. Your breast should completely fill the cup. If it is gapping and the band feels fine, then go down in the cup size.

You don't want to be spilling out of the cup – not from the top, bottom or sides. If the band feels fine then go up a cup size.

If you raise your arms up (do this a few times), the bra should stay against your body, not lifting up or off. If this happens, try a few things:

- Adjust the shoulder straps by loosening them.
- Pay attention to the band. Is it too tight? Or too loose? Or just right?
- If the band is just right, and adjusting the shoulder straps didn't work, then go up a cup size.
- If you have a more petite frame, and you find a bra that fits the band, and you don't quite fill the cup and you have already tried the next cup size down, and it's still not quite right – OR if you have the "right" size, the band fits and you fill the cup, but the wire is poking your underarms, then try a Demi bra.
- A Demi style bra is different from a full coverage bra. The Demi has less wire by about an inch or more.
- Try on different styles of bras. Every style fits and fills different and can "shape" your breast differently.
- If your bra fits correctly, it should NOT be painful or uncomfortable to wear.

EXTRA TIP: if a new bra has an adjustable back band with several hooks, it's best if it fits on the tightest hook. You'll have room to adjust it, when it stretches out, and all bras will eventually stretch due to normal washing and wear.

There you go, yes it is a bit to take in (pun intended). I do hope though, after reading all that, you will know how to find your bra size. That you are no longer freaked out or overwhelmed, or feel resigned to the fact that you will never be comfortable again, to lead a wriggle free life. Instead, that you have a new found confidence in looking for your ladies perfect house..

That's pretty much what it is. There may be a litte time involved but remember put the effort in now and you can forever hold your peace, or should I say they will be forever holding theirs. It will be like shopping for your body shape, now you know it.

Into the store you go, knowing what you need and what you want. It's now all about the fun of choosing what you love. There is such beautiful heavenly lingerie out there, it is waiting to be graced upon your body. When you know your bra size it's just about what fabric, colors, and patterns rock your boat. Then you shout, 'I want this bra, in this size, in every color.' Let's not forget that you will also now be comfortable throughout the day. Oh, the sheer bliss of it. No more writhing and wriggling.

From now on, the tops and dresses you wear will look that much better because of what lies beneath. When you are walking down the street in your fabulous outfit and you have the most divine lingerie on underneath, you will feel amazing from head to toe... from inside out. You won't even realise that you are walking in a way, like you have a sparkling tiara on top of your pretty little head. Just the way you should. You got this girl! You have GOT this!

Enhancing your silhouette

Body shapers are wee-miracle performers. A fast and non-surgical way of looking great in what you are wearing. From super strong control styles that create wow factor change, to designs that reduce the appearance of cellulite.

Shapewear has now become that piece in your wardrobe that is our little cherry on the top – a must. The trouble shooter for your problematic areas. Even though you are now dressing for your beautiful body shape, there will be an occasion when this will add that ultra wow look.

But there are a number of women who are not big fans when it comes to shapewear. They say that it's just so uncomfortable. I agree. Yes it can be if you don't have the right fit, BUT it's not on forever, and it is going to serve a specific purpose. Especially if your outfit is for an event or occasion and it matters what you look like.

Us girls know that sometimes for beauty there is a little pain – right? When we just have to say to ourselves 'suck it up princess!' There are many different weights of shape wear too, you can get the light weight ones, which are way more comfortable to wear. Depending on what and how much you are trying to attack. There are so many options now with styles.

Many women say it's the secret to looking good, as it makes clothes sit where they should and just hang better. Giving you a really smooth outline and fabulous silhouette.

You don't have to worry about VPL (visible panty line) or "back fat" and the "awful muffin top".

They steam roller over all the lumps and bumps. It is not really about making you look thinner, but it definitely helps. Lots of small sized women wear shape wear, even though many think itis just for bigger women. Thinner women can also be far from toned, with curves in the wrong places. They wear them because they say it just pulls things in. For a sharper more toned and "kept together" look.

There are different types of shape wear for different challenging areas. We have:

- The mid-section to create shaping
- Under bust to lift and support
- Compression to lift your tush and limit stomach and back bulge.
- Cellulite control and also thermal weight loss support.

Let's look at them now.

1. For wow factor curve creation, the latex in this type of garment creates strong compression in your midsection. Many garments use different

amounts of latex to create the shaping, the different weights as I just mentioned. So looking for this in the construction of shapewear is something to remember. It will reduce your midsection by one to three inches, immediately allowing you to look up to three sizes more tucked in and smoothed out. Which can, not only give an hourglass figure but greatly reduces any problematic areas. Wow. Worth a try.

2. The underbust shapers go right up to the area just below your bra. This type of shaper does more than just one thing. It supports the ladies, giving an instant lift and a fabulous push up effect. Yippee, with an end result of a leaner, elongated body look.

3. Shapewear is a great compressor and an easy way to get rid of that muffin top and extra bulges. But, while you are wearing a garment for these reasons, the one area you may not want to compress is the tush. Lots of shapers actually have built in designs that are meant to lift your tush, while reducing and eliminating back and tummy bumps and bulges. Sounds good right?

4. Now we have shapewear with built-in weight loss activity. Garments with thermal latex designs can increase thermal activity in the core. They increase the blood flow and move toxins. Studies have shown some sustained loss of inches with long-term results.

Cellulite Control

5. Some of the most effective non-surgical treatments for cellulite come in the form of garments you can wear. Anti-cellulite shapers use techniques like micro-massage with some using infused garments to smooth and create a more even toned skin. It reduces and eliminates the look of the dreaded orange peel look. Again smoothing bumps and bulges at the same time.

Now, with more knowledge of what lies beneath, in the way of shape wear and how it is important. It can make a massive difference to the outward look of that special dress or whatever it may be, for work and play. Imagine, you now know your perfect style of clothing, after learning your body shape and also how to obtain the correct bra. The perfect colors for your skin tone PLUS the kind of shape wear options, to help give you that wow factor with what you are wearing. Tighten, freshen, smooth, lift, enhance and elongate... worth a try my dear....worth a try!

Colors & Skin Tones

How to make your skin pop and glow!

How to look even more gorgeous than you already are — by matching your tones to your colors!

I am so excited to share this wonderful info with you on your tones and colours. It really does make a difference, and people will ask you, what did you do to your skin? What makeup do you wear? How do you get that extra healthy gorgeous glow? Have you been on holiday? It's our little secret... its all about you wearing the right colours for your tones., as simple and easy as that!

Lots of people choose to wear and buy clothes according to the latest fashion trends and styles. This is usually aligned with the seasons. Instead, they should be picking out clothes in colors, based on their skin's natural tones. That's ok, as many are not thinking about their skin tone when out shopping for their next closet addition.

But now you do know. It is like learning what styles you should be wearing for your particular body shape. It really does matter and makes a big difference as you will get that extra pop and glow. It will also help you to choose not only your best colors but also jewelry, foundation, blush, eye shadows, lipstick and hair color.

Some colors can make you look like you have just been to a spa retreat for a week. Others make you look like you need to go for a month. So wearing the wrong color really isn't doing you any favors. It can make your skin look like you need a shot of vitamin D, or you can look like one whole blob of blended color.

Choosing clothing that will complement and enhance your skin tone is not hard. In saying that though, you do need some basic knowledge of color theory (which I give you below), and the ability to determine your skin's undertones.

Choosing the right shades of color for your glorious wardrobe will help you look fabulous, feel confident, and the super plus is that you will actually need very little make-up or accessories to look extra amazing. So what I ask, is not to love?

> The first step is understanding what skin tone and undertone category you are in. Our skin's surface tone is the color that you would describe yourself as having, e.g. (light, fair, medium, light tan, dark tan, etc.). Your skin's undertone is the color underneath the surface. You can have same skin color as someone else, but a different undertone.

When broken down, these are like this:
Cool (pink, red or bluish undertones)
Warm (yellow, peachy, golden undertones)
Neutral (a mix of warm and cool undertones)

Let me say though, there is quite a big misconception that pale girls can't be warm-toned. Yet many fair-skinned women have warm undertones, and dark-skinned women have cool tones.

Skin tone categories:
- Light
- Fair
- Medium
- Light/dark tan
- Dark tan/bronze

Tips on how to discover your tone

1. Blue or Green Veined Girl?

Look at the veins on the inside of your wrist. Are they blue or green? If they look bluer, you likely have cool undertones. If the veins look greenish, you're warm. Ifs worth noting that for warm girl tones, your veins aren't actually green, they look it because you're seeing them through yellow-toned skin (yellow + blue = green).

If your veins are not very visible, find a spot on your body where you can easily see your veins. If they are blue, you have a cool skin undertone. If they're green, then you have a warm skin undertone.

Your notes_____

_____

_____

_____

While a person's skin surface tone may change due to some environmental factors like the weather, your skin undertone or the skin tone that lies right beneath the surface tone will remain constant. Skin undertones are identified as the following:

Warm undertones – described to have peachy or golden yellow skin undertones.

Cool undertones – gravitate towards the bluish, red, and pink skin undertones.

2. Gold or Silver Girl?

Think about whether you look better in silver or gold jewelry (not which you like more, but which actually makes you look more radiant, glowing, and alive). Ask friends to help. Typically, girls with cool undertones look better in silver, white, gold and platinum metals, and warm-toned girls look better in gold, pewter, bronze and copper.

Your notes_____

_____

_____

_____

3. The Neutrals

Think about what neutral shades flatter you the most. Do your skin, eyes and face look more vibrant and healthy in bright white and black hues, or ivory, off-whites, and brown/tan shades? The former means you're probably cool-toned, and the latter, warm.

Your notes_____

_____

_____

_____

4. Eyes and Hair

Your natural eye and hair colors can also help you to figure out your coloring. Customarily, cool people have eyes that are blue, gray, or green and have blond, brown, or black hair with blue, silver, violet and ash undertones.

Conversely, warm-toned women usually have brown, amber, or hazel eyes with strawberry blond, red, brown, or black hair. Their hair tends to have gold, red, orange, or yellow undertones.

Your notes_____

_____

_____

_____

5. What does the sun tell you?

When you're out in the sun, does your skin turn a golden-brown, or does it burn and turn pink first? If you fit into the former category, you're warm-toned, while cool tones tend to burn (fair-skinned cool girls will simply burn, while medium-skinned cool-toned girls will burn then tan).

Your notes_____

_____

_____

_____

6. Are you a celebrity match?

Here are a few celebs who have cool undertones: Delta Goodrem, Scarlett Johansson, Megan Fox, Lucy Liu and Cameron Diaz.

Here are a few that have warm undertones: Halle Berry, Jessica Alba, Jennifer Aniston, Ariana Grande and Kendall Jenner.

Your notes_____

_____

_____

_____

7. What is the color that makes YOU shine?

There's no denying that certain colors will make you look more fabulous, regardless of your skin's undertone. Warm-toned girls should lean toward yellows, oranges, browns, yellow-greens, ivory's, and warm reds, while cool-toned girls should wear blues, greens, pinks, purples, blue-greens, magentas, and true "blue-based" reds.

Your notes_____

_____

_____

_____

Are you a cool, warm or neutral girl

Before you can choose your perfect clothing colors, you'll need to determine your skin tone. Skin tones vary from warm yellow/green-based) to cool (pink/blue-based). Some people have a neutral skin tone that works well with both warm and cool tones.

Test using foundation

Be sure that you don't wear any makeup before doing this test.

Go to a department store and look for the make-up section.

Use the makeup tester to check your skin tone. Look for a shade of warm color, neutral color, or cool color. Apply a small dab of the foundation makeup to your wrist or on your face.

Choose the color that best complements your natural skin tone. Test using metal. Be sure that you don't wear any jewelry or nail polish before doing this test.

On your left wrist or hand, try on a bracelet, wrist watch, or ring in gold material. On your other wrist or hand, wear a silver bracelet, wrist watch, or ring.

A white metal like silver will complement a person with cool skin tone, while the gold metal will look better on a person with a warm skin tone.

Test using paper

Before doing this test, again, be sure that you aren't wearing any nail polish or jewelry. Use a plain, white piece of paper and place your palm and hand on it. Turn over the paper to see your palms and arms.

Check if there is a distinctly blue or pink cast If you see one of those colors, then your skin tone is cool. If you see an orange or yellow cast, then your skin tone is warm.

Test Using Comparison

Comparing your skin tone to others' skin tones could be helpful, they may also want to figure out their own as well. Ask some of your family and friends to stand in front of the mirror. Compare each complexion. Skin tone looks pinker, compared with the others who may have cool skin tone. Next to the others, a person who looks more golden probably is inclined to be a warm color tone.

Tips on how to discover your tone

1. Blue or Green Veined Girl?

Look at the veins on the inside of your wrist. Are they blue or green? If they look bluer, you likely have cool undertones. If the veins look greenish, you're warm. It's worth noting that for warm girl tones, your veins aren't actually green, they look it because you're seeing them through yellow-toned skin (yellow + blue = green).

If your veins are not very visible, find a spot on your body where you can easily see your veins. If they are blue, you have a cool skin undertone. If they're green, then you have a warm skin undertone.

Your notes_____

_____

_____

While a person's skin surface tone may change due to some environmental factors like the weather, your skin undertone or the skin tone that lies right beneath the surface tone will remain constant. Skin undertones are identified as the following:

Warm undertones – described to have peachy or golden yellow skin undertones .

Cool undertones – gravitate towards the bluish, red, and pink skin undertones.

Test Using Yellow Fabric

Get a piece of yellow fabric, and place it beside your face. If you have a warm skin tone, then your complexion will be bright and glowing next to this type of color.

If you are a cool skin tone color, your complexion against this color of fabric will be the opposite. If you want to see a cool skin tone color that looks glowing, try to use a blue color fabric. You will notice that gives a good effect on the cool skin tone color and does the opposite for the warm skin tone color.

Test using white fabric

Another way you can determine your skin undertone is to get some white fabric around your neck and shoulders. If your face looks blue or pink you will most probably be cool skin tone.

If your face looks yellowish or peachy you will most probably have warm skin tone. Neutral skinned people normally look greenish next to the white fabric. Have fun and learn how to match your colors.

You can start mixing and matching colors together for you to wear. A fun way to do this is by using the color wheel. You may look at some colors and think – really? But yes go with it, as they will actually look fab together. That's because of this rainbow color wheel. If you try to create an imaginary line to split the color wheel, half of the color wheel contain warm colors, and the other half are cool colors. There are two main ways to pick colors that will look great together:

Choose a gorgeous color from the heart

Use your finger to trace the color opposite of that color on the Heart to get the color that will complement your first pick. The two colors that you got are called "complementary colors". If they complement one another on the wheel, they will also complement one another in your wardrobe.

Color Heart

Choose another color, look for the color on its left or bight

These are what are called "analogous colors". Remember that half of the color wheel is warm and the other is cool, so you may need to play around with analogous color combos to find ones that match your skin tone.

Colors that make you look fab with any tone

White – can make any skin tone color look good. It does not require any certain color of skin, eyes, or hair.

Blush – can make any skin tone color look beautiful with a glow like no other.

Emerald Green – this happens to be one of my favorite colors. It looks stunning for both skin tone colors, whether you have warm or cool skin tones. For example, Catherine Zeta-Jones and Elizabeth Moss wear the same color, and both of them look gorgeous even though they have different tones.

Red – not only enhances both skin tone colors, it makes you feel confident and powerful.

Eggplant – not everyone likes this color, but eggplant doesn't offer any bad effects on any skin color. Instead it makes any skin tone look good.

Enhance your Complexion with awesome clothing choices!

Fair skin tones

If you have a pale skin tone, it can easily make you look washed out, with the wrong colors.

Look healthy and vibrant and stick to a base of darker colors, such as navy blue, deep brown, black, charcoal, burgundy, and deep green. Avoid soft pastels, light beige and anything else too close to your skin tone, as well as bright colors, such as yellow or orange. Divine, rich, jewel tones combined with lighter hints of camel, slate gray or sand colors, can complement your skin tone rather than bleach it out.

Medium skin tones

Medium skin tones look the best with both light colors and dark or rich colors. Picking colors from opposite ends of the spectrum, such as white, light beige, stone grey, black and deeper jewel tones. Avoid wearing colors, such as light brown, mustard yellow or olive green. If you're on the darker side of medium, you can experiment with brighter, medium-toned colors.

Dark skin tones

Dark skin tones have the most options when choosing clothing, because looking washed out is not an issue. It's still important to be smart when choosing your colors. However, stick with a darker navy blue, black or charcoal as a base for your closet, but add in highlights of bright colors and those gorgeous jewel tones. Stay clear of dark brown, especially if it's similar to your skin tone. Pastel shades also look good on you.

Talk to me!

What skin tone will emerald green complement?

Emerald green will complement and enhance all types of skin colors from dark tone, earth tone to light toned people. It has an extra wow factor on people with an olive complexion, and fair-skinned people with both cool and warm tones.

What clothing color works with a warm skin tone?

The earthy colors of clothing works best for this skin tone. Pick out clothes in brown, red, and green colors. Grey, navy blue, and ivory are also great to complement this skin type.

What is the best fabric color for an olive complexion?

Having a color: grey for an olive complexion is lucky because it means you can wear all kinds of grey. This first sentence doesn't make sense here? The best color for olive skin though is pink. It adds a glow to the person. Shades of the red & orange color group are also complimentary options.

What colors work best with dark skin tones?

The safest color for a dark skin tone is white, but if you want to wear any other colors, you can try shades of purple, pink, accents of soft to rich yellow, copper, gold and bronze. Light colors compliment a darker complexion, such as peach, pale green, pink or orange. These colors will help to enhance a dark skin complexion.

What colors make blushed skin, brown eyes, and reddish brown hair pop?

If you have true auburn, red, or copper hair, you probably have yellowish, ivory, or golden undertones to your skin. If you have one of these hair colors, you might have green, hazel or brown eyes.

For this kind of combo, natural and earth tones suit you best. Brown, dark and olive green, red, orange, gold, and beige look fab on you. Purple, navy, bright bold red, pink, gray and taupe will probably not do you any favours for your overall features.

Universal black will make your face look sunken and sallow. To wear black correctly, you should pair it with one of the colors mentioned above. Your face will glow if you wear a black dress with a jacket in one of the colors that compliment above.

How would a lovely jade color look on browner skin?

Brown skin is a perfect match with bright colors such as: yellow, peach, silver, coral, gold and other rich jewel tones. These colors look gorgeous on a brown skin tone. Jade is one of the jewel tones and looks great on the brown skin tone. Even so, it still depends on how deep your skin tone is.

What colors of fabric compliment silver?

Almost any color, anything can go with silver. If you want to achieve a frosted look, you can try white or blue. Mixing wine/maroon or purple with silver, will give you a regal look. If you're aiming for a more retro look, then try silver with orange or yellow.

How do you enhance a warm skin tone?

If you want to complement warm colored clothes, combine them with cool ones. For example, blue and green, pink and yellow, blue and yellow. The warm colors are highlighted when paired with cool colors.

Warm tones are attractive when combining with earth colors, as long as they're not too orange in color. If you mix warm tones with something that's more on the orange side, it would be a bit too much on the eye. Also, warm tones do not blend well with very dark shades, especially blue, because the dark colors will bleach out the warm ones. Lighter pastel colors will work better.

Is an orange color a good match for cooler tones?

Yes! Orange goes well with cool tones. You can team it with a dark color like black, which will make your skin tone look brighter and gives that extra glow we all love to have.

Cobalt blue is best for which complexion?

All complexions will work great with cobalt blue, as it is a lighter color and will show or pop better than any other darker color.

Phew... You have had a lot to take in, but like learning your body shape and the styles that you should wear, you just need to do the same with your color. Once you know your colors as well, you will have it all. You will be wearing the perfect styles and clothes for your body shape AND the perfect colors that will make you stand out and shine like a diamond.

Imagine going shopping with all that ammunition! Could be time for a color raid in your closet soon!

Your notes_____

_____

_____

_____

I do hope this will help you to understand your tones and colors a little better, so now you have that little extra something, that little extra glow about you... I mean why not look even more fabulous then you already are?!

Style Fact File

What you need to know to look fabulous!

We are going to talk layering. Wearing loose and tight, your tush, jean styles, and outfit ideas. So let's get started!

A loose fitting piece over a fitted piece can look gorgeous when paired with the right garmtent. This style is one of my all-time favorite looks. I always feel chic when I wear my fitted jeans and a classy white blouse with a bang of color (from the accessories). Of course, let's never forget the pumps, for that extra superlicious pop.

Styling tips

Go for thicker fabrics for fitted pieces and a flowy draping fabric, like rayon, silk or chiffon for the looser ones.

Change up your loose dress

Just because your dress is a little big, it doesn't mean you have to chuck it out. Find a cool patterned belt or one with bright colors, depending on the fabric of the dress. Pop a belt around your waist and pull out some of the material so it gently hangs over the belt. Or sit the waist down on the hip more and do the same if that suits your body shape better. If you have a shift style dress and just want to wear it a different way, do the same for a whole new vibe. But remember, that adding a belt must be right for your body shape, so check your notes.

Marry up loose tops with tight pants

If you want to wear an oversized top or sweater, wear leggings or skinny jeans. If you want to wear harem or leisure-style trousers, wear a tighter top/shirt or jacket.

A flowy draping blouse as mentioned, is always a pretty fabulous thing, especially when paired up again with skinny jeans or leggings. Don't wear a loose top or loose bottom as you will look like a sack has been dumped upon you. Yes, not a great visual..

Wear a super cute blazer over your relaxed fit dress

This will give you a whole new look. Full length or knee length. Any loose fabric around the waist gets nipped in when you button down a blazer, giving you a great silhouette and creates a waistline that flatters your shape. I personally love a one button blazer and prefer a slightly more cropped look. But remember to work with your rules for your body shape.

Blazers and crop jackets are always a great addition to many outfits for the cooler months, always giving a posh vibe for that top layer when you need it. This would have to be my go-to top layer.

Skinnies + loose tops = super cool, cute and chic

Skinnies are a very popular go-to cut, pairing them with flowy blouses and longer tunics for the perfect balance of shape and proportion. Look for the darker wash denim styles for a slimming silhouette. Or depending on your body shape, you could go for the lighter wash.

Loose fitted but with a great cut buttoned shirt, married with the right color of skinny jeans for your body type is another fab look. For a cute and casual outfit, try a pretty, relaxed fit blouse with a pair of dress shorts for a sassy night look with strappy heels. Or keep it casual for day wear with a pair of denim or chino style shorts with sandals or pumps for a perfect easy to wear look.

You can also pair this with a casual black skinny or distressed look jeans.

Another great option is tailored pants for the evening. I love the look of either a white blouse with a pop of color from the accessories, or go for a bright block shirt, or a pretty pattern with subtle accessories.

What I find so comfy and super cute, is a button down shirt with a crop top over the top with just the bottom and the collar poking out, along with the shirt cuffs. Paired with skinnies and pumps, it's cool, classy and a casual favorite of mine. Jeggings. They look just like a pair of jeans, but are soft and stretchy when you want a legging feel but a jean look. These have been very popular. An oversized top and boots is another casual comfy look.

Your lace dress from the warmer months can also work for autumn/winter when you pop on a cute cardigan, tights and cool boots. This is a rather adorable girl next door look.

Pair a relaxed fit sweater over another relaxed fit top, add skinny jeans and a funky pair of ankle boots. If you have block color tops add a print scarf to bring it all together. Wear cool high socks under high boots and over leggings, paired with a tank top and a short blazer. A casual adorable and slightly playful look. I tend to go for the tank tops with the scooped hem, which don't cut straight across sharply, and has a soft edge look to it. When paired with a cropped blazer that does go straight, it gives some visual layering interest.

Choosing loose linen trousers and pairing it with a fitted cropped top is an elegant look.

If you have a bigger style top, wear something short on the bottom. And if you're wearing something loose on the bottom, pair it with something that shows off your arms, chest, shoulders, or back. It gives balance.

I love the look of a loose fitting top with a slightly wider neck so you can wear it as a slash neck or off one shoulder for a really sassy but chic look that shows a little bit of skin. Then wear it over a tight mini skirt or tailored shorts or leggings/jeans. Or do the opposite and wear looser on the bottom and something on top that shows a little skin, as just mentioned.

A tunic-length top in a bold block or statement print is another super comfy and stylish outfit for a lazy mood completed with either pumps or sandals depending where your day is taking you. I am a complete sucker for heels and totally in love with them. For me that outfit would be a no-brainer with the pumps, wherever I was going.

Maxi skirt + tee + jacket

Maxi skirts are great. You can get your fitted styles or your looser gathered look ones. Both styles look fab with your fav tee and a crop jacket for when you need that extra layer. Super cute.

Oversized sweater tunic

A cool tunic sweater will look awesome with leggings, jeggings, skinnies or tights. Boot socks sitting just above a pair of knee boots. Also cute with ankle boots. I find a funky ankle boot, whether it be a pattern or cool color, is something I always find myself wearing to give that extra push to an outfit. This tunic sweater look can be a lazy boho style but still a chic look.

Knit sweater

A knit loose fit sweater in a soft pastel – looks effortlessly stylish and pretty, matched with either jeggings or leggings in black or grey. I have always loved baby pink and grey. A scarf with some pattern and knee or cute ankle boots and you're good to go.

Layer me up and layer me right!

Layering is so versatile and fabulous and totally changes a look when done right. It is also great when moving from day to night and changing temperatures.

Here are some tips.

- Layering is versatile and practical and can also look chic all at the same time. You have to get it right though to carry the look off. It gives you a brand new look and style and also covers you for the changing.
- Choose the right inner layers. Start with a basic, lightweight top (a solid neutral or striped may do) Keep the under-layers more fitted to keep your slim shape.
- Wear outer layers that can be easily added or removed. Layer a cardigan, shirt or crop jacket over a fitted top for a personal and stylish look, mix different fabrics – have fun and create your own personal style.

Using color

Think about your colors when layering, it is essential for creating a look that is cohesive and feels connected. You don't want to look like there should be a performing monkey on your shoulder.

Layer on the layers

Several layers of knits that work with your body shape is a warm and attractive way of layering, then add a fun color or patterned scarf. Mix your textures don't be scared to play with texture and mix it up a little. It isn't a good look to have all of the same, especially with texture. Create visual interest. You learnt already with the body shape chapter where and where not to add the visual interest.

Leather looks

Leather is great because it is warm without being heavy and thick. There are some amazing quality faux leather around. If you go down that route, make sure it is a really good quality. It will then sit right and won't look cheap and ill fitting. It will add elegance.

Avoid multiple bold patterns that overlap

You can wear multiple patterns in one outfit, just remember to give them some space. So you are not wearing a colliding chaotic ensemble.

Pick your lengths

Same lengths are prone to look heavy and can also be unflattering. When layering always try and go for different lengths. For example; if I am wearing skinny jeans, shirt and a cropped jacket with pointed front, I will go for a straight across or scooped hem top or shirt that is longer than the jacket. I just love cropped jackets so I wear them often – even if just a little, I will normally have the under garment peeking out to some degree. Layering can also be flattering and slimming when done right.

Scarves are a great way to achieve a layered look. There are so many options and they give that extra sparkle to any outfit. Bold block colors, pretty or dominant patterns, and prints. They have a sophisticated look about them. I especially love them with a blazer. They just tie in and complete a look in a simple way. Taking a lazy outfit into one of chic interest.

Accessorize

It is always the detail and the finishing touches that complete a full look. Even just a gentle light accessory can make all the difference. I love gold so have my favorite chunky gold curb link bracelet and a plain gold bangle. I find between the two I can make them work for many outfits, and also married together.

I have never liked heaps of accessories so I tend to stick to simple pieces. If I need something with some "wow" I tend to go for a bright color rather than anything too fussy.

This is just my own personal preference. It can be very different of course when I am dressing my models for the runway! I also wear bigger earrings and no necklace, or a necklace and no earrings. It is easy to go overboard with them and de-rail a look.

Using accessories are so important though, just like the icing on the cake with a cherry on the top. It brings it all together. Just think about it as you go.

So there we have it, you now have some tips and ideas on layering and matching your loose and tight. Have fun and create your own style. It's what fashion is all about!

Looking WOW in your jeans!

Let's talk about jeans – our super comfy go-to pants, with so many styles and so many cuts. Which are best for you? Let's start with stretch.

Stretch jeans are made out of a type of denim cotton (or cotton/polyester blend) that incorporates a small percentage of elastane, a stretchy, synthetic fiber, also known as spandex, or lycra, into the fabric.

When shopping for either stretch or rigid jeans, you will know by now, you must look for a pair that works for your body shape as well as giving thought to the stretch factor.

Stretch jeans normally include about one to three percent elastane. If you are between jean sizes, it's a good idea to buy stretch jeans in your smaller size, as they will most probably loosen up after a few wears. Remember, stretch jeans are meant to fit you snugly.

If you are not sure, try sitting down. You will know soon enough. If you can sit without getting cut in half, or feeling a degree of muffin top, you should be good in this size.

If you are a plus size, you may want to shop for a body contouring skinny jean. Most of the brands carry jeans for the curvaceous body. How stretchy you want the jeans is totally up to you. The combinations below are assuming the stretch is combined with a high quality denim.

1% stretch – a great jean to contour your body, with just enough stretch to make you look fab while still being comfy. This is my personal preference.

2-3% stretch – once again a great contouring jean, at the same time even more comfortable. These you could wear anytime and anywhere.

4% stretch – this one is a super comfy and super figure hugging, for an all-around jean for work and play.

So you see, it is a personal choice. Go with how they feel and think where you would mainly wear them and what they would be for. I have different jeans depending on what I am doing and where I am going. I have rigid ones and a little stretch through to the maximum stretch. Skinnies and straight legged. That's me though, some people will happily having one pair of favorite jeans for everything.

You will know when you put them on, it's either a yeah-nuh, or it's asking the sales girl to cut off the tag cause you are wearing those babies out the door!

Time to talk about your tush....

You know you want your butt to look fabulous...

When buying a pair of jeans, one of the first things you do when trying on a pair is to turn and check out your butt in the mirror. That's because you already know the right jeans can do magnificent things back there – the wrong ones can make it look... well pretty bad. Let's be straight up.

Even though jeans are a casual look, if you know how to wear them they can be classy and sexy.

My all-time favorite look is a pair of skinny or straight cut jeans, soft draping shirt, a blazer if cooler, and a pair of vibrant or patterned pumps. Hello... in love right there!

The back pockets are pretty crucial and DO matter. They can significantly change how your butt looks in a pair of jeans. We all have wonderful shapes and wonderfuly shaped butts. Like the rest of our body shape though, we have to learn how to cover them in the right way to make them look as super-hot as can be.

Let's talk tush shapes. It's always a fun read with me huh? As you may already know there are contoured jeans you can get with the butt lifters and molders, etc. built in. If you want to know what and how to wear a standard pair of jeans, here you go.

Is there even a butt there – do you have a flat looking butt?

Pick flap pockets, don't do the rigid denim.

Steer clear of the boyfriend styles of jeans – their relaxed fit can make it look low and even flatter.

Try the styles with flap/bulkier pockets to add interest, detail, and volume.

Go for tighter-fitting styles to give you some shape and lift your tush up.

The lighter denim and the ones with the washes, pattern and prints will give some oomph to your tush. It deceives the eye. You may remember this from when we learnt our body shapes.

Are you bubbling out at the back?

Stay away from small back pockets, they will accentuate the seat area.

Don't let them high ride and don't let them go too low either. Medium rise.

They need to fit snugly but non-gaping at the waist.

A contoured seam just above the back pocket should nicely hold in your curves.

Keep it simple, no interest and detail will work best.

Do you have a wider load at the back?

Do not wear wide-leg jeans. They just grab you at your widest part and that's about it.

The back pockets really need to be positioned close together, visually it will give you a thinner looking tush.

Keep them simple and go for jeans with basic, mid-size back pockets.

Don't choose flap pockets, bulk or detail. We don't want any visual interest back there.

Plain, plain and more plain.

Wear the darker washes, no light washes.

Does your butt hang low?

You must have pockets. If there are no pockets it will seem to hang even lower.

We want pockets that are positioned higher up, it draws the eyes upwards not down.

The bottom of the back pockets can't be lower than the bottom curve of your butt (where your cheeks meet your legs). If they are, you have turned into a pancake.

Don't go for the boyfriend style jeans; you want to look for tighter-fitting jeans. Your butt will look like it is on the ground. Not a good look.

Do you have a curvaceous butt?

If you want to slim down the look of those curves behind, don't add bulk or detail or interest.

Keep simple and flat.

No flap pockets, they just add oomph.

Pockets that will enhance your butt and make it look best are larger, plainer back pockets that are quite wide and are positioned lower.

You really need to try and find jeans with pockets that start mid-way down your butt, and end at the tops of thighs.

Do you have a butt shaped a little like a triangle?

A triangle butt is basically when your widest part is where your hips meet up with your thighs.

You must get strategic with the position of the pockets. You want ones that are on a diagonal or sitting higher toward the waist, this will draw the eyes to the middle of your tush, not on the outside of your thighs.

So there you have it and now you know what will give you an amazing looking tush

Let's talk jeans styles now

The Skinny Jeans

These are a popular jean as they flatter quite a few body shapes.

Super fitting and designed to accentuate your shape and follow those lines.

They are cut in from the hip to the ankle, giving you an elongated look and are super easy to style up or down. My personal favorite.

The Boyfriend Jeans

Designed to shadow menswear, boyfriend style jeans are one of the loosest and most relaxed cuts out of all the styles.

The relaxed fit and totally worn-in look, are super comfy and cool favorite.

These were originally inspired by women who liked to borrow their boyfriends' clothes, and have become a real favorite style.

They fit loose from the hip to the bottom and normally sit a little lower on the waist.

They are usually distressed and just plain washed.

The Trouser Jeans

These are pretty much the wider-leg jean with a tailored cut. Great and easy to style. They normally have a higher rise and are fitted through the hips and cut wider through the rest of the leg, with the widest point at the hem.

A great style jean for bigger thighs

They are comfortable to wear and flattering to the shape.

Trouser jeans have a classy look to them.

The Straight Cut Jeans

These jeans are just as they sound and are cut straight from the hip to the hem.

I love this cut of jeans also, they are so versatile and can be worn with just about anything. Having a simple, classy look to them, they are also comfortable to wear.

They are a great fit; tight but not too tight, loose but not too loose.

The straight cut pairs well with just about everything in your wardrobe.

The Boot Cut Jeans

Boot-cut jeans normally have a lower-rise waist and are cut slim through the thigh, subtly flaring from the knee to the hem. They are designed to fit around boots, hence the name.

These are our main jean styles, so hopefully you now have a little more knowledge around shopping for the jeans that suit your shape, so you can look and feel wow!

So you now have some info on a little bit of everything to help with styles, so have some fun!

Shopping Tips

How to shop fun and easy!

My shopping tips, ideas, and advice

Of course, we all have our totally impulsive shops where one minute we are at home and the next we find ourselves driving to the mall. Don't we? Well for me that was some time ago now as everyday I get to shop in my own shop! We have all had those shops alone and with friends.

BUT if you have a "need" list and you are on a budget, I would advise a planned option. When are you going? Where are you going? What do you need? How long do you have?

Dress in something chic and classy of course, but also a garment that is easy to get in and out of.

List what to buy. I am a list maker so a "what I need to buy list" is a great idea if there are certain things you are looking for and want to stay focused. Also, it is a help if you are on a budget you need to stick to.

Make sure you are fed and watered before going. There is nothing worse than being on a roll and having to stop because you're starving and starting to fade. Bad and impulsive decisions are made on an empty stomach and when you are a little flat. This could also involve having to dash out to the letterbox to get the credit card bill before hubby gets there first!

Remember to put some fuel in your tank so you can keep on going, like the Duracell bunny battery.

Think about who you will take shopping with you. It also depends on the type of shopping trip it is. You will know who of your friends is best for a specific shop. There is most often THAT friend who you love ever so dearly, and is your total partner in crime but is not quite so practical to work through a list with you.

If you have the option, shop in the mornings, as it is normally less crowded, the racks are full, nice and tidy, and the sales associates have just had their coffee! Lunchtime shopping is always chaotic as everyone is out and trying to squeeze in a shop before going back to work.

If a particular item catches your eye, try it on. As now you know what body shape you are, you will only be scanning for certain styles. If you find ten things in your style for your shape. Take them all in, it's part of the fun.

Don't hesitate to ask for assistance from store people.

If it doesn't rock your boat, don't get it. Don't settle, you will fall in love with the right thing.

Don't just get something because it is BOGO (buy one get one free, etc.).

If you can't decide between the red one and the blue one and they are right for your body shape, get them both if you can. You want options in your new body shape closet, we don't want you starting back to old styles if you don't have enough.

Don't be afraid to try different sizes until the fit feels and looks right. All brands have different sizing so don't just assume if it isn't in your normal size the game is over. Try another size in the same brand to be sure. It's about the fit, not the size.

Save receipts. Check store's return policy just in case you get it wrong.

Shopping solo is a great idea when you want to feel you have the freedom to go into all the stores you want to go in. if yyou have specific things you need to get, you may find it easier to do it alone

As fun as it is having the girls with you (and you love them to death), you don't always get to go into every store you want to.

Only buy clothes that are your body shape styles and are comfortable, no matter how cute they are or how much they are marked down. Don't be tempted! Remind yourself what you need to be shopping for. Then there is no chance of guessing and being tempted by old habits. That's why you have this guide!

If you want to be super organized and maybe get in on a few sale commercial items shopping out of season is a great way to do it. As you probably already know there can be some great new season sales early.

If a few days have passed, and you can't stop thinking about that one piece you didn't buy, you are having some "should have" moments, go back and get it. It has your name all over it. Life's too short to not get what you love.

Lastly, but most importantly, HAVE FUN!

Now you know your body shape and the styles to look for, it's easy. No more aimless wandering around each store, rifling through the racks, flick, flick, flick, trying lots of things on that didn't fit you right and then walking out as flat as a pancake because you found nothing you liked. Then on top of that, as you tried on all the wrong styles that did not flatter your body, you are now feeling yuk about your body too. NO MORE GIRL. You have got this, remember all we have talked about.

Before you know it, you will be walking out of that store swinging bags of delicious, heavenly new garments, in your perfect colors, and your perfect styles. All you have to do now is throw open your closet doors and hang those treasures up and plan your next date to wear them!

Your notes

Your notes_____

Your notes

Your notes_____

Your notes

♥

Well beautiful people, I do hope you now have a better understanding of your own gorgeous shape. What loves it and what doesn't, and remember no matter what size you are, every single shape has parts that we need to be aware of, has parts that we may love less then others but they are ours.

They have our name on it, made for us, to be cherished by us, to be adorned with the most beautiful things. The red cherry on the very top though, is knowing how and what so that cherry can shine like no other!

That's why my passion for styling holds hands with my passion for designing. Don't forget to pop this pretty little number inside your bag, so you have it when you need it most and above all have fun shopping! With much love,

I love hearing from you so if you want to reach out:

- ⓕ ChristinaKilmisterAuthor
- ⓘ @christinakilmister

- ⓕ LilikaDesignsFashionHouse
- ⓘ @lilika_designs
- 🌐 www.lilikadesigns.com

What You Need To Know For A Fantastic Chic Life

♥

Sisterhood this is for you!
Your simple and easy to use fashion guide,
plus a ton of insider designer tips.

You my gorgeous friend deserve to look
and feel amazing!

With love Christina x

*"This book helped me so much,
I wish I had it 30 years ago!"*

Maria Sullivan, USA.

Christina Kilmister
"Empowering the sisterhood through Fashion"
www.lilikadesigns.com

www.ingramcontent.com/pod-product-compliance
Lightning Source LLC
Chambersburg PA
CBHW040742020526
44107CB00084B/2847